KNIGHTS AND CASTLES

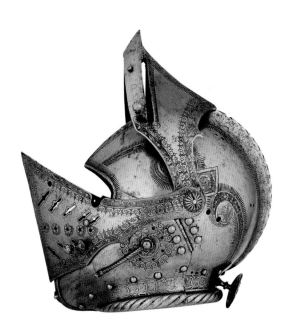

FIRST EDITION
Series Editor Deborah Lock; **US Senior Editor** Shannon Beatty; **Editor** Radhika Haswani;
Senior Art Editor Ann Cannings; **Art Editor** Kanika Kalra; **Producer, Pre-Production** Nadine King;
Picture Researcher Sakshi Saluja; **DTP Designers** Neeraj Bhatia, Dheeraj Singh;
Managing Editor Soma Chowdhury; **Art Director** Martin Wilson;
Reading Consultant Linda Gambrell, PhD

THIS EDITION
Editorial Management by Oriel Square
Produced for DK by WonderLab Group LLC
Jennifer Emmett, Erica Green, Kate Hale, *Founders*

Editors Grace Hill Smith, Libby Romero, Michaela Weglinski;
Photography Editors Kelley Miller, Annette Kiesow, Nicole DiMella; **Managing Editor** Rachel Houghton;
Designers Project Design Company; **Researcher** Michelle Harris; **Copy Editor** Lori Merritt;
Indexer Connie Binder; **Proofreader** Larry Shea; **Reading Specialist** Dr. Jennifer Albro;
Curriculum Specialist Elaine Larson

Published in the United States by DK Publishing
1745 Broadway, 20th Floor, New York, NY 10019

Copyright © 2023 Dorling Kindersley Limited
DK, a Division of Penguin Random House LLC
23 24 25 26 27 10 9 8 7 6 5 4 3 2 1
001–333444–Apr/2023

All rights reserved.
Without limiting the rights under the copyright reserved above, no part of this publication may be reproduced, stored in or introduced into a retrieval system, or transmitted, in any form, or by any means (electronic, mechanical, photocopying, recording, or otherwise), without the prior written permission of the copyright owner.
Published in Great Britain by Dorling Kindersley Limited

A catalog record for this book
is available from the Library of Congress.
HC ISBN: 978-0-7440-6759-0
PB ISBN: 978-0-7440-6760-6

DK books are available at special discounts when purchased
in bulk for sales promotions, premiums, fundraising, or
educational use. For details, contact: DK Publishing Special Markets,
1745 Broadway, 20th Floor, New York, NY 10019
SpecialSales@dk.com

Printed and bound in China

The publisher would like to thank the following for their kind permission to reproduce their images:
a=above; c=center; b=below; l=left; r=right; t=top; b/g=background

123RF.com: andreykuzmin 24tl (shield), Jose Alfonso de Tomas Gargantilla 30tl, Anton Ivanov 37cra, Dmitriy Tereshchenko 28tl;
Alamy Stock Photo: Ann Ronan Picture Library / Heritage-Images / The Print Collector 29tr, Paul Doyle 37tr,
imageBROKER / GTW 41tr, The Picture Art Collection 27tr, 40tl; **Depositphotos Inc:** estebane 38bc; **Dreamstime.com:**
Andreykuzmin 31tr, Serhii Bobyk 24cla, Dauker 14cla, Dmitry 20tl, Ilkin Guliyev 22crb, Vladimir Korostyshevskiy 25tr,
Vladimirs Poplavskis 22tl, Srlee2 17tl, Lazarenka Sviatlana 22clb, Vladvitek 7tr, Vlastas 21tr, Jeff Whyte 44-45b, Witr 19tr;
Getty Images: Prisma / UIG 23tr; **Shutterstock.com:** Miguel Almeida 14crb, badahos 26cla, Danita Delimont 8tl,
Larisa Dmitrieva 38tl, IR Stone 18tl, Nicholas E Jones 42-43, Kozlik 24tl, Patrick Messier 44tl, St. Nick 4-5, ZGPhotography 6tl

Cover images: *Front & Spine:* **Shutterstock.com:** kontrymphoto; *Back:* **Shutterstock.com:** Lemberg Vector studio cra

All other images © Dorling Kindersley

For the curious
www.dk.com

KNIGHTS AND CASTLES

Rupert Matthews

CONTENTS

- **6** Protecting the People
- **14** Great Castles of the World
- **22** Mighty Knights
- **30** Military Monks
- **38** Castles at War

46 Glossary
47 Index
48 Quiz

Castles Everywhere
During the Middle Ages, people built castles all across the world. A castle could only defend the land within a small area. So, rulers built multiple castles to expand their realms.

PROTECTING THE PEOPLE

Castles were built to show power and protect people during times of trouble. When danger threatened, people took their valuables into the castle until the danger had ended. During a war, a castle would be filled with people from the nearby farms seeking protection. Even in peaceful times, castles provided protection from bandits and criminals.

Most castles were built between the years 950 and 1500. This period of time is often called the Middle Ages or medieval period. The design of castles changed over the years. As new weapons were invented to attack castles, new methods of defense were developed, too.

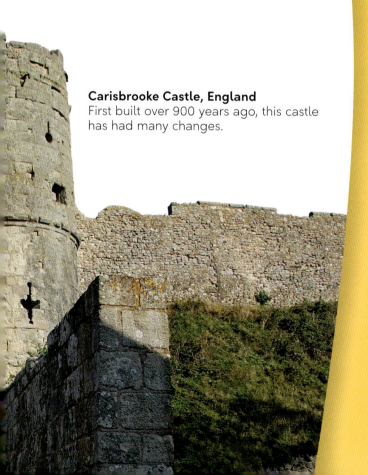

Carisbrooke Castle, England
First built over 900 years ago, this castle has had many changes.

A Home, Too
A castle was also a home. A couple called the lord and the lady took care of a castle. During times of war and peace, they managed and protected their lands, their household, and the many people who served beneath them.

Castles were often built on top of hills or beside rivers to make them more difficult to attack. Some castles were built beside a town to help defend it from enemies.

Early castles were made of wood and earth. A large mound of earth called a motte [MOT] was constructed up to 65 feet (20 m) tall and 200 feet (61 m) wide. On top of the motte was a wooden tower. This was the strongest part of the castle.

Fort or Fortress? These castles don't look like what we might think of as castles. They were much simpler, but they could be built quickly to take control of the land.

Walls in About a Week
These early castles could be built in just eight days.

How to Build a Motte-and-Bailey Castle
1. Choose the site for the castle.
2. Hire a master builder to design it.
3. Hire 300 workers to build it.
4. Dig the ditch around the bailey, and use the soil to build the bank.
5. Build a wooden wall around the bailey.
6. Build buildings in the bailey.
7. Dig a deep ditch around the motte, and pile up the soil to form the motte.
8. Build a tower on top of the motte.
9. Sit back and relax. You are now safe from your enemies.

Beside the motte, a large area of ground was surrounded by a ditch and a bank of earth. A wooden wall was built on top of the bank. This area was called the bailey. Several different buildings might be placed inside the bailey. Soldiers lived in barracks, while horses were kept in stables. The bailey might also include a church, offices, courthouse, workshops, kitchens, or a great hall.

During peaceful times, castles were used for many different purposes. People went there to pay their taxes or to obtain justice from the courts. Criminals would be kept in prison inside castles. Valuable goods would be kept inside the storerooms. More than a hundred people might live inside a castle.

Windsor Castle, England
The keep of this castle was rebuilt as the Round Tower in 1170.

Pricey Protection
Keeps were expensive and took many years to build.

After about the year 1100, the wooden walls and towers began to be replaced with stone. Defenses of stone were stronger and could not be set on fire so easily. Instead of a motte and tower, some castles had a massive square stone tower called a keep. The keep could be over 80 feet (24 m) tall.

Rochester Castle, England
Built in 1127, this tower keep has three floors.

GREAT CASTLES OF THE WORLD

Soon, a new type of castle began to be built. Earth and wood were out. The new castles were made entirely of stone. They were some of the greatest castles ever built.

These new castles were safe. Their stone walls were tall enough to stop attackers on ladders from reaching the top. The walls were so thick that missiles thrown at them from catapults had no effect.

Ready, Aim, Fire!
A catapult was a machine that could launch weapons like rocks or hot tar at a target. The chosen weapon, called the payload, was placed in a bowl-like area of the catapult called a bucket.

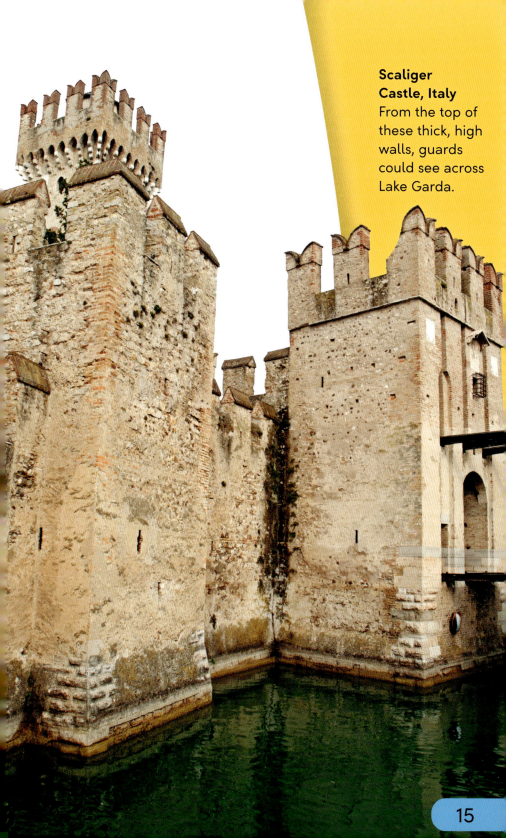

Scaliger Castle, Italy
From the top of these thick, high walls, guards could see across Lake Garda.

On top of the walls were rectangular openings called crenellations. Defenders could hide behind the tall parts of the wall or use their weapons through the gaps in between.

A Place to Hide
A castle's walls could also have wooden platforms that hung out over the side of the castle. The platforms were called hoardings. They had holes at the bottom that allowed defenders to drop heavy rocks onto attackers below without being seen.

The walls had tall, narrow holes in them called arrowslits. Guards standing inside could shoot arrows through the arrowslits. The openings were narrow to stop attackers shooting arrows back through them. Some openings had a short, horizontal slit to allow the guard inside a better view of the attackers.

Himeji [HIM-e-gee] Castle, Japan This fortified castle, also known as White Heron, was completed in 1609. It has more than 80 buildings spread out across multiple baileys. The buildings are connected by a series of gates and a maze of winding paths. A six-story tower stands in the center. The castle is surrounded by thick walls and a double moat.

arrowslit

Murder Holes
Tucked in the ceiling above the gatehouse, these openings allowed defenders to attack anyone who made it past the gatehouse.

Challenge Number One
A moat was the first obstacle that attackers would face when trying to invade the castle. To get past the watery trench, they would have to fill it with dirt or build bridges.

The gate in the outer wall was guarded by a gatehouse. A tall tower protected each side of the gate. A heavy grid of wood called a portcullis could be dropped to block the gateway.

A wooden platform called a drawbridge might cover a pit in front of the gate. The drawbridge was lifted when the gate was closed.

portcullis

Sometimes, a barbican was built outside the gatehouse. This building was like a small castle with walls and towers. Enemies had to capture the barbican before they could attack the gatehouse.

Many castles were surrounded by a deep trench called a moat. Some moats were flooded with water from a nearby stream or spring.

- **Fasil Ghebbi [fa-SIL ge-BI], Ethiopia**
  King Fasil (Fasilidas) established this royal compound, which resembles a medieval European castle, as a permanent capital in 1636. Up until the 19th century, it served as the royal residence for Ethiopia's leaders. Over time, the compound grew to contain some 20 palaces and a host of other royal buildings.

moat

**Lal Qila
[lal KEE-la],
India**
This palace city, called the Red Fort, was built in the middle of the 17th century by Shah Jahan, one of the most famous Mughal emperors. It is surrounded by—and named for—its massive, red sandstone walls.

Later castles had lower walls outside higher walls. These are known as concentric castles. Guards on the inner walls could shoot arrows over the lower walls at the enemy. If the attackers captured the outer walls, the inner walls were still above them.

Caerphilly [CAR-filly] Castle, Wales
Built between 1268 and 1271, this is the earliest concentric castle in the UK.

Many castles had one tower that was taller and had thicker walls than the others. This was the keep or donjon [dun-jun]. It was the strongest part of the castle and would be the last section to be captured by attackers.

Forest Fortress
Château de Vincennes [VAHN-sen] in France had a donjon tower built around 1337. It is 170 feet (52 m) high.

Defensive Design
The high inner wall of Caerphilly Castle in Wales was surrounded by a low outer wall.

Brave in Battle
Knights were the medieval military. Charged with protecting a lord's castle, they had the most dangerous of jobs.

Weighty Warrior
As many as 200,000 iron rings were used to weave a knight's suit of chain mail armor. This metal mesh could stop a sword from slashing their skin.

MIGHTY KNIGHTS

In some parts of the world, honored warriors called knights defended kingdoms and did their ruler's bidding. When King Robert the Bruce of Scotland lay dying in 1329, he asked his trusted knight, Sir James Douglas, to take his heart on a trip to the Holy Land so it could be presented before God before it was buried.

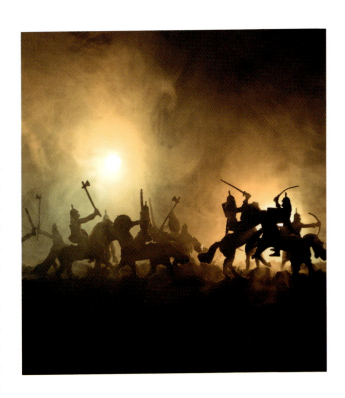

After the king died, his heart was placed in a silver necklace that Douglas wore around his neck. But before Douglas and his company of knights could set out on their holy quest, they were sent to Spain to fight against Moorish armies. Douglas was killed during battle. He and the king's heart were returned to Scotland for burial.

The Moors
This medieval Muslim civilization originated in North Africa. In 711, the Moorish forces invaded the lands now known as Spain and Portugal. They ruled there until they were defeated, almost 800 years later. The Moorish culture—filled with art, science, technology, architecture, and learning—still influences the region today.

School Days
A boy left his home at about the age of seven to begin training for knighthood. He would become a servant, called a page, in a castle. Along with daily chores, he would get a basic education and learn manners. He would play with other pages and begin to learn how to battle.

During the Middle Ages, when castles were built, society was divided into three groups: the farmers and craft workers, the priests and bishops, and the king and his knights. The knights were organized in a strict order of importance. Squires were training to be knights, while bannerets were senior knights.

All knights were expected to obey a code of behavior known as chivalry [SHIV-al-ree]. Knights had to be brave in battle, but gentle in peace. They were supposed to protect the innocent and punish the guilty and be especially kind to women and children. Knights were expected to serve their king faithfully and respect the Church and God's teachings.

Sir John Chandos (c. 1314–1370)
Although not very good at fighting, Chandos was highly skilled at organizing an army.

The Norse
These fierce warriors came from Scandinavia. Children learned to fight from an early age. Wrestling was a favorite sport, and the Norse excelled at hand-to-hand combat. In battle, they fought with spears, axes, and swords. They used big, round, wooden shields for protection. The Norse were also excellent shipbuilders. They used their boats to conduct raids on other countries.

Some knights were not born into nobility. John Hawkwood was the son of a tanner in Essex. In about 1340, he became a soldier and joined the English army invading France. In 1356, he fought so well at the Battle of Poitiers that the King of England, Edward III, made him a knight.

When peace was arranged between England and France, Hawkwood formed a private army of unemployed soldiers, which he named the "White Company." Hawkwood marched his army into Italy and hired out his soldiers to whichever nobleman would pay him the most money. Hawkwood and his men made huge sums of money, and he married a wealthy duke's daughter.

A Head Start
It cost a lot of money to outfit a knight with armor, weapons, and a warhorse. That's why knights usually came from noble families who could handle the price tag.

Sir John Hawkwood (c. 1320–1394)
This is Hawkwood's funerary monument in Florence Cathedral, Italy.

Mighty Warrior
Tomoe Gozen was said to have been a female samurai, or *onna-musha*, during the 12th century. Known as a fearless and ruthless leader, she led a large army during the Genpei War.

The Samurai
From the 10th to the 19th centuries, Japanese feudal lords hired elite warriors called samurai. Samurai were skilled with both the bow and the sword.

The Mamluks
This group started out in the ninth century as an army of young enslaved males. They overthrew their owners and created their own empire, ruling Egypt and what is now Syria from 1250 to 1517. During that time, the warriors also defeated two other great armies, the Mongols and the Crusaders.

"El Cid," meaning "The Lord," was the nickname of a heroic Spanish knight, Rodrigo Díaz de Vivar. He was born in 1040 into a noble family in the Kingdom of Castile. In 1065, King Sancho of Spain made El Cid his standard bearer. Carrying the flag, El Cid bravely and skillfully led the army into battle, fighting against the Moorish armies of southern Spain.

However, in 1081, the new king, Alfonso, quarreled with El Cid and sent him into exile. El Cid captured the Spanish city of Valencia [va-LEN-see-ah] in 1094 and declared himself ruler. When he was killed in battle in 1099, his wife, Jimena, had his body strapped to his horse so he could lead one last charge.

Rodrigo Díaz de Vivar (c. 1040–1099)
Rodrigo Díaz de Vivar, known as El Cid, was a Spanish knight who became a Spanish national hero.

Charge!
Knights carried long spears called lances when fighting from atop their horses. When knights fell from their horses during battle, they had swords at the ready.

Rich Rewards
As payment for their military service, knights were given their own land and a noble title. Some of the most successful knights became more powerful than the lords they had served.

MILITARY MONKS

Some castles were built for an unusual group of monks, who fought like knights. They were called the Military Orders of Monks.

In 1119, the French knight Sir Hugues de Payens found the bodies of a group of pilgrims near Jerusalem. They had been murdered by bandits on their way to the holy city.

Hugues founded a group of fighting monks called the Poor Fellow Soldiers of Christ. Their job was to patrol the roads to protect the pilgrims.

Code of Conduct
The Knights Templar followed a strict code of rules. They were not allowed to wear fancy clothes. Even shoelaces were forbidden.

King Baldwin of Jerusalem gave buildings on the Temple Mount in the city to them, and these monk-knights became known as the Knights Templar. For 200 years, they built castles, including the huge Kerak Castle, and fought battles in the Holy Land (now Israel).

Sacred Symbol
The symbol of the Knights Templar was a white shield with a red cross.

Kerak Castle, Jordan
Begun in 1132, it has cliffs on two sides.

Around the year 1120, the monks of the Order of St. John of the Hospital also took up arms to protect pilgrims to help them reach the holy sites. These Knights Hospitaller built many impressive castles to defend the route. Rebuilt in 1186, Margat Castle with its round towers perched on top of cliffs became their greatest castle.

Warrior Teen
Joan of Arc (c. 1412–1431) was a French peasant with no military training. Yet she led the French army to a great victory in the city of Orléans. A few months later, she was captured in battle. She was tried and convicted of crimes against the Church. As punishment, she was burned at the stake. In 1920, she was named a Catholic saint. She is known as the Maid of Orléans.

Margat Castle, Syria
Also known as Marqab, this castle was triangular-shaped with a steep drop on one side.

The Knights Hospitaller also had a navy to protect pilgrims traveling by sea from attacks by pirates. They built castles on islands along the Mediterranean Sea as command posts, such as Kolossi Castle on Cyprus in 1254. They later ruled Malta until 1798, and today, they are based in Rome, Italy.

Kolossi Castle, Cyprus
Just one large tower now remains.

In 1190, the Order of Teutonic [too-TAH-nic] Knights was founded in Germany to protect pilgrims traveling to the Holy Land. In 1220, these knights bought the village of Mi'ilya and built Castellum Regis with its four massive square towers and a small church inside. In 1229, a tall narrow ridge became the site of Montfort Castle, their headquarters in the Holy Land.

Malbork Castle, Poland This castle has been enlarged several times and now covers 52 acres, making it the world's largest castle.

From 1230 onward, the Teutonic Knights fought wars against people in eastern Europe who weren't Christian. Malbork Castle, now in Poland, was built in 1274 as their world headquarters. By 1400, the threat had disappeared, so the order became involved in charity work instead.

As well as the three great Military Orders, there were lots of smaller ones. The Order of Aviz was founded in 1146 to protect the Kingdom of Portugal against the Moorish armies. The Order of Calatrava fought from 1164 to 1490 to reconquer Spain from the Moorish troops. The Order of the Dragon was founded in Hungary in 1408 to fight the Turks.

Saone Castle, Syria
Saone Castle is thought to be one of the strongest castles in the world, but in 1188 it fell after a siege of just three days.

All of these Military Orders had a large role in the Crusades, which were religious wars between Christians and Muslims.

Armies from Christian countries in Medieval Europe felt that the city of Jerusalem and the surrounding Holy Land belonged to Christians. They waged war on the Muslim people who lived there. Crusaders rebuilt small forts, such as Saone [SONE] Castle in Syria, into huge, strong castles.

Beaufort Castle, Lebanon
Called the "Beautiful Castle," Beaufort was held by the Knights Templar until 1268.

Krak des Chevaliers [shuh-VAL-ee-ay], Syria
This castle began as a hilltop fortress. With walls up to 80 feet (24 m) thick, it was considered impossible to invade. The Knights Hospitaller rebuilt it into a great castle between 1142 and 1271.

Battering Ram
A tree trunk tipped in iron was placed on a wagon and wheeled forward to smash castle walls.

CASTLES AT WAR

In 1136, Sir Baldwin de Redvers, Earl of Devon, rebelled against King Stephen of England. The king marched his army to lay siege to de Redvers's castle in Exeter. The king's army built a wooden castle to protect them, and they surrounded Exeter Castle to block supplies from reaching de Redvers and his people. The attackers used siege weapons to smash the walls of the outer bailey. They also dug a tunnel under the East Tower, causing it to collapse. De Redvers finally surrendered after dry weather caused the well to go dry.

Slingshot
The trebuchet was a giant slingshot. It could hurl enormous rocks and barrels of hot tar as far as three American football fields.

At Siege
A siege began with a blockade. Attackers surrounded a castle, making sure that no one could come out or in.

Nicola de la Haye Saves England
At a time when women had few rights, Nicola de la Haye inherited her father's land and his position as Constable of Lincoln Castle when he died. In 1217, French and English rebels overtook much of England. They tried to take Lincoln Castle. But, led by de la Haye, the castle did not fall. After reinforcements arrived, the attackers were defeated. This allowed the English king to remain on the throne.

A Long Battle
A siege could last months or even years.

When a siege took place, a castle became a very busy place. Hundreds of people from nearby farms and villages would come to the castle for safety, bringing their belongings. Tents and sheds were put up in the bailey along with large numbers of farm animals, carts, and tools.

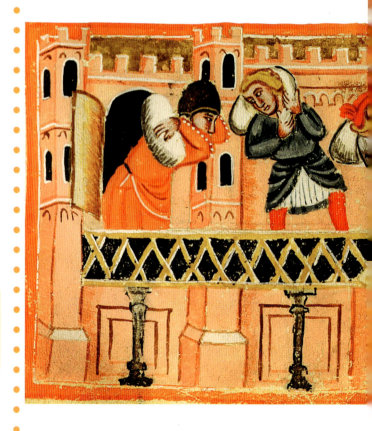

The knight who owned the castle had to prepare for a siege. He brought huge amounts of food into the castle's storerooms. He made sure his soldiers had plenty of weapons and equipment. Riders on fast horses were sent out to look for the enemy approaching. When the enemy was seen, the gate was locked shut. No one could leave, and no further supplies could come in. The soldiers guarded the walls, ready to fight.

Water
Castles had containers called cisterns that could catch rainwater. This gave defenders under siege enough water to drink. Some castles had an underground well for water, too.

Supplying Provisions
This picture on a manuscript from the 1300s shows supplies arriving at a castle.

A Seven-Year Siege

The defenses of Harlech Castle in Wales were so strong that attackers tried to starve their targets into surrender. But supplies could still reach the castle by sea. The seven-year-long siege (1461–1468) only ended when an army of 10,000 men attacked and the outer defenses fell.

The siege of Kenilworth Castle lasted longer than most. It began in January 1266 when King Henry III attacked rebels led by Henry de Hastings. The wide moat surrounding the castle meant that the king's siege towers were useless and the catapults' stones could not reach the castle walls.

King Henry brought barges to carry his army over the moat, but they were sunk by the defenders of the castle. An effort to cross the water by raft also failed. Finally, an envoy from the Pope in Rome arranged a peace deal, and the rebels surrendered in December 1266.

Kenilworth Castle, England
This castle later became a splendid palace in the 1500s.

A Long History
Edinburgh Castle is the most besieged place in Great Britain.

Neither side in a fight ever wanted a siege to last long, but both wanted to win. In 1341, Scottish nobleman William Douglas set out to attack Edinburgh Castle, which was being held by the English. One night, Douglas led 1,000 soldiers to hide in trees near the castle. At dawn, 20 men pretending to be merchants drove a wagon to the castle. They said they brought food to sell.

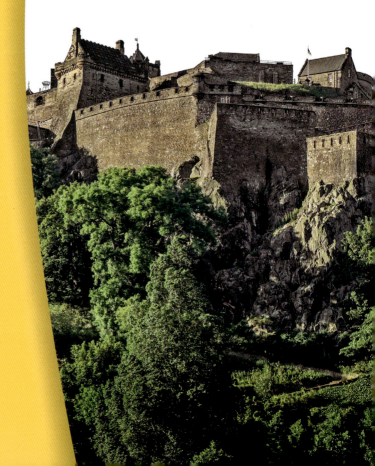

The English opened the gates to let the "merchants" in. Dozens of Scottish soldiers were hiding in the cart. They leapt out to defend the gate and keep it open until Douglas arrived with his army to burst in and capture the castle.

Edinburgh Castle, Scotland
This castle was built on a tall volcanic crag.

GLOSSARY

Bandits
A group of robbers or people who break the law

Barbican
The tower and walls that form an outer defense of a castle

Catapult
A weapon that throws large stones

Concentric
[con-SEN-tric]
Circles of different sizes with the same center

Crenellations
[KREN-el-lay-tions]
Battlements with regular gaps

Envoy
A messenger or representative

Exile
Being unable to live in one's own country

Funerary
Used to remember a dead person

Headquarters
The main offices from where an organization is controlled

Horizontal
Flat or level, going from side to side

Moors
A group of Muslim people with African and Arab ancestry

Pilgrimage
A journey to a sacred place

Pilgrims
Religious people who travel to a sacred place

Pope
The leader of the Roman Catholic Church

Portcullis
[port-KULL-is]
A strong, heavy gate made from iron or wooden bars with points at the bottom, which hangs over a gateway into a castle

Siege
[SEE-j]
When an enemy surrounds a town or building, cutting off supplies and trying to force those inside to surrender

Standard
The flag of a royal family

Tanner
A person whose job is to make animal skins into leather

Taxes
Payment that has to be made to those in authority

Trench
A long, narrow hole dug out in the ground

Valuables
Small objects, such as jewelry, that belong to someone and are worth a lot to them

INDEX

arrowslits 17
attackers
  castle defenses 14, 16-17, 20-21
  sieges 42, 44-45
bailey 10, 38, 40
bandits 6, 30
bannerets 24
barbican 19
battering ram 38
Beaufort Castle, Lebanon 37
building a castle 10
Caerphilly Castle, Wales 20
Carisbrooke Castle, England 7
catapults 14, 42
Chandos, Sir John 24
Château de Vincennes, France 21
chivalry 24
cisterns 41
concentric castles 20
crenellations 16
Crusades 37
de Hastings, Sir Henry 42
de la Haye, Nicola 40
de Redvers, Sir Baldwin 38
defenses
  arrowslits 17
  barbican 19
  castle walls 20-21
  concentric castles 20
  crenellations 16
  hoardings 16
  keeps 12, 13, 21
  location 8
  moat 18, 19, 42
  murder holes 18
  stone towers and walls 12, 14

donjon 21
Douglas, Sir James 22-23
Douglas, William 44-45
drawbridge 18
Edinburgh Castle, Scotland 44-45
El Cid (Rodrigo Díaz de Vivar) 28, 29
Exeter Castle, England 38
Fasil Ghebbi, Ethiopia 19
forts and fortresses 8
gatehouse 18, 19
Gozen, Tomoe 27
Harlech Castle, Wales 42
Hawkwood, Sir John 26, 27
Henry III, King of England 42-43
Himeji Castle, Japan 17
hoardings 16
Hugues de Payens, Sir 30
keeps 12, 13, 21
Joan of Arc 32
Kenilworth Castle, England 42-43
Kerak Castle, Jordan 31
Knights Hospitaller 32-33, 37
Knights Templar 30, 31, 37
Kolossi Castle, Cyprus 33
Krak des Chevaliers, Syria 37
Lal Qila, India 20
lances 29
lord and lady 7
Malbork Castle, Poland 34, 35
Mamluks 28
Margat Castle, Syria 32, 33
Military Orders of Monks 30-37

moat 18, 19, 42
monks 30-37
motte 8, 10, 12
murder holes 18
Moors 23, 28, 36
Norse 25
pilgrims 30, 32, 33, 34
portcullis 18
Robert the Bruce, King of Scotland 22
Rochester Castle, England 13
Samurai 27
Saone Castle, Syria 36, 37
Scaliger Castle, Italy 15
siege 38-45
slingshot 38
soldiers
  barracks 10
  monks as 30
  private army 26
  sieges 41, 44-45
squires 24
standard 28
Stephen, King of England 38
tanner 26
Teutonic Knights 34-35
towers
  barbican 19
  collapse 38
  gatehouse 18
  keeps 12, 13, 21
  motte-and-bailey castles 8, 10
  round towers 12, 32
  siege towers 42
  square towers 12, 34
Windsor Castle, England 12

47

QUIZ

Answer the questions to see what you have learned. Check your answers in the key below.

1. What was used to make early castles?
2. Why were arrowslits narrow?
3. Where did the Moorish civilization originally come from?
4. What was the strongest part of a castle?
5. What was a deep trench that surrounded a castle called?
6. Who was asked to carry Scottish King Robert the Bruce's heart to the Holy Land?
7. Which military order of monks used Margat Castle?
8. True or False: Sieges always ended quickly.

1. Wood and earth 2. To stop attackers from shooting arrows back through the wall 3. North Africa 4. The donjon or keep 5. A moat 6. Sir James Douglas 7. Knights Hospitaller 8. False